SOCIAL MEDIA MA

Hotel Industry Edition

Reach Online Prospects & Turn Them Into Offline Clientele In 21 Straightforward Steps

Camilla Carboni

Create-The-Dream

SOCIAL MEDIA MARKETING: Hotel Industry Edition
Reach Online Prospects & Turn Them Into Offline Clientele
In 21 Straightforward Steps

Copyright© 2013 by Camilla Carboni, Create-The-Dream

ISBN-13: 978-0-9912031-0-9
Printed in the United States of America
First Printing: November 2013
Cover Design: Camilla Carboni

Trademarks

All terms mentioned in this book that are known to be trademarks or service marks have been appropriately capitalized. Camilla Carboni cannot attest to the accuracy of this information. Use of a term in this book should not be regarded as affecting the validity of any trademark or service mark.
Facebook® is a registered trademark of Facebook Inc.
Twitter® is a registered trademark of Twitter Inc.
Flickr® is a registered trademark of Flickr Inc.
Pinterest® is a registered trademark of Pinterest Inc.
TripAdvisor® is a registered trademark of TripAdvisor LLC.
SocialOomph® is a registered trademark of SocialOomph, Inc.
TweetDeck® is a registered trademark of Twitter Inc.
HootSuite™ is a registered trademark of HootSuite Media Inc.
ReviewAnalyst® is a registered trademark of ReviewAnalyst LLC.

Dedication And Acknowledgements

For the millions of Resort, Hotel, Motel and Bed & Breakfast Owners and Managers worldwide, this one's for you. May this step-by-step guide assist you in transforming your online presence, advancing your reputation and attracting and retaining guests.

To my Mom Joan, thank you for encouraging me to pursue my dream of writing. Though I find myself now without adequate words to express my gratitude for having you as my mother - know this – you are my earth angel.

To my Daps and Grans who watch over me from above, thank you for all you taught me. You inspire my writing.

To my boyfriend Matt, thank you for your ongoing love and support and for putting up with my writing obsession.

To my loving cat Bruce, who sits beside me as I write, thank you for teaching me unconditional affection and for reminding me to take breaks.

To my writing accomplice Melissa, thank you for sharing my passion and contributing to this journey.

To everyone else who has been a part of my life and writing passage, thank you for the many ways you have moved and motivated me.

Contents

Illustrations

"One of the greatest challenges companies face
in adjusting to the impact of social media,
is knowing where to start."

~ Simon Mainwaring

Introduction:

Going Social is Essential

Social Media Marketing is a pivotal part of engaging consumers in our 21st Century world. Consumers spend a great deal of their time online each day, and you need to be where your consumers are. Quite simply, if you want to sell your property effectively in today's society, you must be present on social networks and utilize them to establish awareness for your property online.

Hospitality and the Hotel Industry specifically are no exception. Fortunately, the very nature of social media makes online marketing a particularly responsive medium for the hospitality industry. Various social networks can be utilized to engage, connect, share imagery and create a dream-like experience for prospective, current or past consumers, so that they will desire to visit, or return to, your property and ultimately live the dream that you have pieced together for them online.

"Increasingly, consumers don't search for products and services. Rather, services come to their attention via social media."

~ Erik Qualman

Whether your property is a multi-story resort or a family run bed and breakfast, a well-positioned, implemented and maintained social media campaign can significantly enhance your property's marketing reach. By interacting with connections online, you are engaging potential consumers. As you converse, share relevant content and provide a glimpse into what your property offers, you are revealing your property to the social media world and creating presence where presence already is. Best of all, other than the time involved in creating and maintaining your property's social media presence, you gain vast online exposure with a zero dollar investment.

Follow the 21 Steps outlined in this book and watch as your individual property's online exposure grows rapidly and reaches a vast target audience.

We will begin by gaining a broader understanding of the type of audience you should cater to online and how to engage with this audience to soft sell your property. As we proceed through the chapters, we will cover specific social media marketing tactics as well as the creation of a Social Calendar. I will also share best practices, tips and tricks to gaining the online reach necessary to convert online connections into offline customers.

Chapter One:

Clarify Your Pitch

Before you even begin to target an online audience, you first need to understand what attracts guests to your property.

In this Chapter we will cover the three fundamentals of effective marketing:

- **Understand Your Audience** – define your audience
- **Categorize Effectively** – target your audience
- **Create-The-Dream** – capture your audience

Step 1: Understand Your Audience

Before exposing your property to the masses online, make sure that your audience is well defined. If you have already launched your social media campaign – *don't worry and don't skip this section* - we will work together to fine tune your target audience.

This step is vitally important. *Critical actually!* If you do not cater to the correct audience for your property, you will not benefit from the power of social media marketing. Why? Because no matter how good your campaign may be, if you are pitching to the wrong audience, you will not convert your connections into guests.

Keeping that in mind, let's begin.

Do a little research on your clientele. Chat with your Revenue Manager, your Director of Sales and your General Manager. Determine why, at what cost, and how often most guests choose to enjoy your property.

Compile a character sketch. Once you have completed your research and are clear on the type of guest your property attracts and sustains, piece together a guest character sketch.

Think of this as the equivalent of what an author would do to conceive a fictional book character; or a method actor would do to better understand the motivation behind his role.

Your character sketch should include basic demographics, such as age range, gender breakdown percentage, educational standing, employment status, average income, geographic location and anticipated lifestyle, at a minimum. *Get specific!* The more specific you are the better you can master your audience and how to communicate with them.

Let's work through this step together. I will begin by providing two examples of what this should look like.

Example One

Your property is an exclusive and modern mountain-side resort with 160 guest rooms. The average daily rate is $320. The average length of stay is three nights. You sell the majority of your guestrooms through your resort's website as well as through Luxury Link. Your spa is featured in Conde´ Nast as one of the best in the world.

Your resort is a year round destination because of the fame of the location and reputation of the property, but your peak season is winter, when international skiers frequent your hallways.

Your property is in business because you offer an experience of a lifetime that ignites all five senses and promises adventure.

This example property's Character Sketch Worksheet would look something like this:

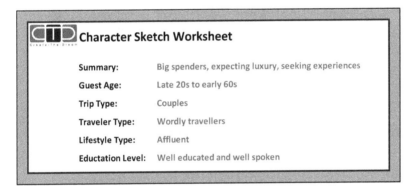

Figure 1.1.1. Character Sketch Worksheet Example One.

Example Two

You have a semi-renovated hotel in the city center with 72 rooms. The average daily rate is $95. The average length of stay is one night. You sell the majority of your guest rooms on Hotels.com. Your property is not a commodity, nor does it drive much press; it provides convenient and central stopover accommodation.

Your hotel's location is accessible by tourists wishing to visit and explore the city at a reasonable rate.

You are in business because you provide affordable, comfortable accommodation to the family and business traveler.

This example property's Character Sketch Worksheet would look something like this:

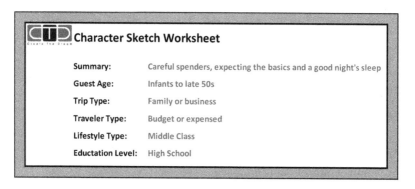

Figure 1.1.2. Character Sketch Worksheet Example Two.

Visit camillacarboni.com to access blank Character Sketch Worksheets to complete this exercise for your property.

Step 2: Categorize Effectively

Only move to this step once you have a fully rounded character sketch in place. I know what you're thinking – "all my guests don't fit into one mold" – and you're right, they certainly don't. Like any marketing campaign, however, you have to identify the most common characteristics of your guests' personality and lifestyle. Then focus on those in order to appeal to the majority of your target audience.

Let's dig deeper into how to *Categorize Effectively* by beginning with examples of what *not* to do. These examples should clearly demonstrate the importance of categorizing and how doing so incorrectly can isolate prospective guests from your marketing campaign.

Example One

Your property is luxurious and attracts the lavish spender.

You want to place a $1.99 breakfast banner in your lobby. You are going to use this same image as your Facebook Cover picture and you are planning on tweeting about the offer each day.

While we all like a good deal, you would likely not appeal to your exclusive audience by marketing this $1.99 breakfast offer. This audience, as a stereotype, desires an adventure. They would rather pay more for an exhilarating experience.

Example Two

Your property is a budget roadside motel.

You are about to redo your display cases and are thinking of showcasing Louis Vuitton. You also like the idea of placing a 5% discount card for Ruth's Chris Steak House in each guestroom keycard packet and pinning this promotion to your Pinterest page.

While designer brands are well known throughout society and everyone is grateful for a discount coupon, this audience would likely have appreciated and responded to the $1.99 breakfast deal far more than the Louis Vuitton display and the 5% discount card for Ruth's Chris Steak House.

To market effectively you must cater to what your audience feels most comfortable with *and* what they are ultimately seeking. When an audience is comfortable they feel at ease and understood; in turn, their desire to pursue your property is heightened.

Step 3: Create-The-Dream

Think of your property as delivering an experience. View it as a destination, a landmark, a once in a lifetime adventure. *How would you describe it? Why is it appealing? What attracts your guests?*

It is essential to determine what makes your property desirable. Without a desire for your property, you simply cannot and will not be able to tap into the power of consumer marketing psychology, which is necessary in order to turn your property into a recognizable brand and drive sales. I therefore coined the marketing term "Create-The-Dream".

A brand does not exist if consumers do not desire it. So, once you have uncovered the desire behind your property, there are numerous proven steps you can take to communicate this desire, or dream, to your audience.

Creating the dream is a notion I believe to be fundamental in successfully capitalizing on your online marketing campaign.

Why Create?

You might ask why I used the word "Create" in "Create-The-Dream". It's a great question with a very precise answer:

Your audience relies on you, or your marketing team, to piece together an experience for them and present it in a form that is complete and enticing.

Take Coca-Cola for example. Established in 1886, it remains the world's most recognizable brand. Coca-Cola's marketing team are masters of experience branding. Take a moment to think about their advertisements. Just about every one you see, whether it is a TV commercial, a radio clip or a billboard, presents a scene in which a personality feels incredible as they take a sip of ice-cold Coca-Cola. This imagery is by design. The product is formulated and marketed as a refreshing experience. It goes well beyond just a drink. It's desirable, appealing and psychologically stimulating. We can see ourselves as the personality; we can live the experience. It stimulates our senses and we want a sip of Cola-Cola!

Why Dream?

And what about the word "Dream" in "Create-The-Dream," you might ask. Well, if you look up dream in any dictionary you will find definitions like these:

Dream [dreem]

Noun: a cherished hope; ambition; aspiration

Verb: to have an image or fantasy about

Adjective: desirable; ideal

It is no secret – it is a fact – we all dream, we all hope, we all fantasize and we all desire. It should therefore come as no surprise that our customers do as well. *And that's the beauty of it!* To market effectively we really just need to place ourselves in our customers' shoes. Think about what would entice you to visit your property if you were them. *Is it the location? Is it the amenities? Is it the price point? Is it the prestige? Is it the dining? Is the service? Is it the activities?*

Once you understand what it is that makes your property desirable, you simply have to replicate this in your marketing. That is what I mean when I say "Create-The-Dream" for your customers.

Chapter Two:

Refine Your Image

When you are clear on who your target audience is, what they are comfortable with and what makes your property desirable to them, you are ready to begin refining your property's image.

To do this, there are three foundational steps that must be addressed. These steps will ensure that your marketing reflects the dream you need to create in order to convert online connections into offline guests.

They are:

- **Define Your Brand Voice** – identify your style
- **Consider Your Property 'Packaging'** – formulate your identity
- **Create A Seamless Transition** – consider all touchpoints

Step 4: Define Your Brand Voice

Brand voice is crucial and it goes hand in hand with *Understanding Your Audience* and the need to *Categorize Effectively*. Think of your brand voice as if your property were talking aloud to your customers. Ask yourself how they would like to be addressed, what they would feel comfortable with and what they would enjoy talking about.

I like to use the Queen and surfer example as a stereotyped distinction of the importance of appropriate colloquialism, tone and style.

Imagine that the Queen of England arrives in Hawai'i. She steps elegantly out of her private jet into the blazing Hawaiian sunshine. Her embroidered suit sits tight around her bodice and her collar is starched stiff against her neck. With her satin glove she dabs a glisten of moisture from her forehead before she reclines gracefully into her limousine for her drive to the North Shore. Upon arrival, she departs her limousine and glances out toward the ocean, admiring its raw beauty. Suddenly, a local surfer, with his dripping wet board shorts and golden tan, rushes beside her carelessly. Noticing her enticement with the ocean, he turns to her and grins in his carefree manner before attempting to gain her as a surf lesson client: "Wanna hit the waves, brah?"

The Queen is stunned and has no idea what was just said to her. She feels quite uncomfortable and out of place. She shakes her head indifferently and returns to her vehicle.

Now, I spent three and a half years in Hawai'i and deeply appreciate the relaxed culture, so this is by no means a discriminatory distinction. It quite simply illustrates the misunderstanding and lack of conversion that results when you do not cater to your audience correctly.

Had the surfer spoken the exact same phrase to another surfer, there would have been no confusion and most likely the offer would have been accepted. Similarly, had the surfer addressed the Queen in a manner she understood, perhaps by saying "good afternoon Madam, may I entice you to join me for a surf lesson?," the Queen's response would likely have been far more positive.

It is important to note that neither method of communicating is incorrect, it is just a matter of communicating in a manner that is appropriate to the audience you are addressing. Doing so will enable you to gain the results you desire.

Communication with customers online is no different. You should communicate online in the same manner, style and tone that you would face to face with a VIP guest. (And really, in the hospitality industry, you should treat every guest as a VIP guest).

Think carefully now about what style and conversation type would be appropriate to your clientele. **Your online voice must be an accurate extension of your property's offline offerings and ambience.**

The Brand Voice Worksheet will assist you in honing in on your appropriate brand voice. You can locate a copy by visiting camillacarboni.com. As an example, I have completed the worksheet based on the audience profile in Chapter One's Character Sketch Worksheet (Figure 1.1.1).

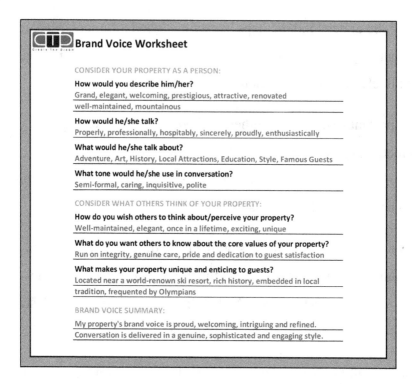

Figure 2.4.1. Brand Voice Worksheet.

Once you have completed the questions on the worksheet, take time to summarize the style of voice you need to be using in order to most effectively portray your property. Share this summary with anyone and everyone in your business or organization that may be contributing to online interactions. It is vital to ensure that your brand voice is consistent so that the dream you are creating for your audience is never deconstructed.

Step 5: Consider Your Property 'Packaging'

Keeping brand voice in mind, let's take it one step further and work to define your property 'packaging'.

It's no secret that every detail communicates. There have been numerous books and theses written about the subject, explaining the importance of the look, feel, taste and smell of a product and how even one incongruent element can lessen the experience of your brand.

I vividly recall attending a business lunch at a very prestigious restaurant in Honolulu. This restaurant's reputation was top-notch and I was very excited to experience it. I had a pre-established expectation in my mind and, as I entered, the well-kept décor and stylish settings certainly lived up to that. The waiter greeted us very professionally and handed each of us a menu. He then placed a linen napkin over his right arm and, with his left arm tucked behind his back, he began pouring me water…into the dirty, cracked glass at my table setting. I was mortified.

Sure - it can happen anywhere and it does - the point is that every single detail of your guests' experience must be considered. One tiny thing that doesn't seem to fit with the property image can tarnish a guest's perception and hurt the property's reputation.

Use the following worksheet found online at camillacarboni.com to begin considering the two most important aspects of property 'packaging':

- The impression that you hope to leave guests with;
- The expectations you think your guests have of your property.

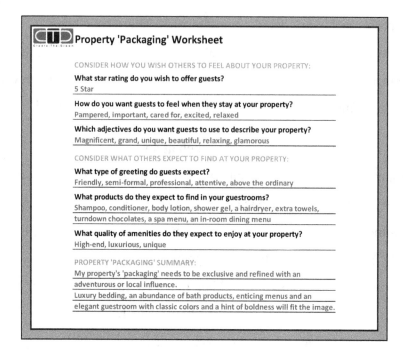

Figure 2.5.1. Property 'Packaging' Worksheet.

Your property 'packaging' needs to align with the dream you are presenting online in order to successfully market your property to your target audience. Once you have identified the reputation you desire and the probable expectations of your guests', think about what type of branding, imagery, colors, linens, restaurants, bath products, in-room menus etc., will help you to create this dream. List these thoughts in the summary section of your Property 'Packaging' Worksheet.

Step 6: Create a Seamless Transition

Keeping in mind that every detail communicates, you cannot have anything contradict or potentially break your customers' experience or feeling about your property. You must carefully consider every detail of your campaign and how it interacts with itself. In doing so, always keep in the forefront of your mind the touchpoints that your guests will experience once they take initiative to book a night with you.

Touchpoints are any and every interaction that a guest has with your property.

The below diagram provides a visual example of some of the primary touchpoints to consider in the Hotel Industry.

Figure 2.6.1. Common touchpoints in the Hotel Industry.

Understanding the impact such touchpoints have on the overall image of your property is important.

The pre-booking experience, which includes online interactions, must be a seamless extension - a prelude - of what can be expected at your property. Keeping that in mind, we can now begin our online marketing journey.

Chapter Three:

Develop Your Online Brand

Now that you have your target audience defined and your brand image refined, it is time to build your online presence.

Begin with your website. It is the heart of your online presence and it must embody the dream you are trying to create. It is so important that this Chapter is dedicated solely to this one step:

- **Perfect Your Website** – Create-The-Dream online

Step 7: Perfect Your Website

Many of you will already have websites up and running. If you do not, now is the time to create one.

Your website must capture everything that is desirable about your property. It must be a complete overview (both in words and imagery) of what your property has to offer.

Think of your website as your core customer facing platform; the pulse of your online presence from which all else extends and returns. It needs to link, lead to and support everything else you are going to do with your online campaign. It must be visually appealing, informative, on brand and directed at the audience you have identified as the target audience for your property.

It may be helpful to dedicate an hour or two to do a little research. Stop in at your local Barnes and Noble and browse through the website design section, or Google websites or website templates in the Hotel Industry. Pay close attention to your first impression of the websites you research. Examine their content, layout and voice. You will start to notice that some websites are very effective and well thought out, while others simply would not entice you to book accommodation.

The following illustrations demonstrate how a website's marketing copy and color scheme can either break or create-the-dream behind your property.

<u>Note:</u> these examples are fictional and for demonstrational purposes only.

Example One – Breaking the Dream

Figure 3.7.1. Website Example One – Breaking the Dream.

Jarring colors, inappropriate or badly phrased copy, sloppy tone and grainy images do not capture the right audience for this 5 star property, nor do they entice any audience to further pursue the property.

Example Two – Creating the Dream

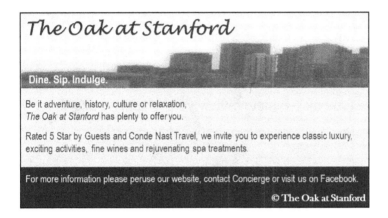

Figure 3.7.2. Website Example Two – Creating the Dream.

Classic coloring, well-versed marketing copy, polite tone and softened imagery attract guests likely to visit this property. While it is still a very simple and concise homepage, this version is a seamless extension of the luxurious property and entices the audience to learn more.

***

Many people make the mistake of thinking a website is merely a portal of information for customers. I'm here to tell you that it's far more than that. It's the face of your property; it is where your potential customers go to decide if they want to visit your property or not. *Your website is a huge deal!* It needs to sell your property so convincingly that, after viewing your site, your audience will want to book accommodation immediately.

When you start to think of your website in that manner, you will start to notice things that you could change or improve to enhance your potential customers' online experience.

Consider the following action items as you work toward perfecting your website (you may want to review your Character Sketch Worksheets from Chapter One to support this process):

- **Examine the color scheme.** Is it in keeping with your property's décor, landscape and image?
- **Scrutinize the imagery.** Do your photographs look professional? Are they enticing?
- **Check your content.** Is it is well-written, informative? Is it consistent with your brand voice?
- **Focus on flow.** Is your website easy to navigate? Do all the links work? Is it a seamless experience?
- **Pretend you are your audience.** Does your website cover and provide the imagery and information that your typical audience member would likely expect and look for?

It is also good idea to ask someone who is removed from your business, (and who will be objective and honest), to review your website once you have completed the above steps. Share your audience profile and ask them to provide you with feedback on the following items:

- Does the website cater to the target audience?
- Does the content and imagery entice you to become an offline customer?
- Was the website user friendly?
- If hypothetically you were a tourist looking for information, could you find enough detail about the location and attractions that you would not have to leave the website?

Pay attention to their feedback and adjust your website accordingly. Often the objective eye can point out an important change that makes all the difference in effectively marketing your property online.

Once you are sure that your website is a perfect reflection of your property, begin extending the reach of your online message through social networks, as detailed in the next chapter.

Chapter Four:

Take it Social

The reason it is so important to perfect your website before beginning or refining your social presence, is because every online network you utilize should be a seamless extension of your property's chosen brand image. With your website finalized, you should have a color scheme, imagery, content and layout already defined for your brand. Your brand image is defined. Now, all you have to do is continue this look and feel on Facebook, Twitter, Flickr, Pinterest, TripAdvisor and any other social networking sites you think would benefit your property and reach your respective audience.

What follows is a step-by-step guide on how to get started on each of the abovementioned sites.

Step 8: Setting Up Your Facebook Page

Allow 25-45 minutes to complete this section.

a) Visit **facebook.com**.

b) Beneath the login and sign up information is a button which reads "Create a Page". Click it.

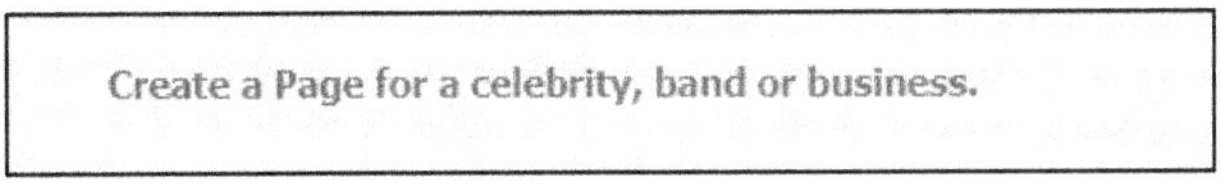

Create a Page for a celebrity, band or business.

Figure 4.8.1. First step to "Create a Page" on Facebook.

c) Select the type of Page you wish to create. In most cases in the Hotel Industry, this would be the "Local Business or Place" option.

Figure 4.8.2. Page types on Facebook.

d) You will then be prompted to fill in a location. This is vitally important in enabling your potential customers to locate your property. You will also be asked to place your Page into a category. Select "Hotel" in the "Choose a category" dropdown list shown below.

Figure 4.8.3. Basic information required for Facebook pages.

e) Once you have completed the above steps and agreed to the Facebook Page Terms, you will be prompted to either join or log in to your personal Facebook profile. You must have a personal Profile in order to have a Facebook Page.

f) After logging in you will be asked to provide some basic information, including a description of your property and your website URL.

In the description, be sure to write a compelling and descriptive overview of what your property offers and include keywords for search engine optimization purposes. For example, if your property attracts skiers, include the words "ski," "mountains," "snow" and the name of the landmark location where your property resides.

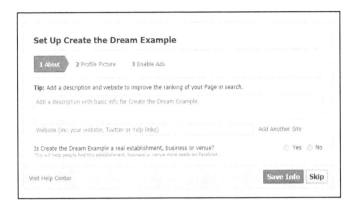

Figure 4.8.4. "About" section of Facebook Page set up.

g) Click "Save Info" and you will be prompted to upload a Profile Picture, the second step shown in Figure 4.8.4. Make sure the image you choose is high resolution, clear and enticing to prospective consumers.

h) Next you will be asked to "Enable Ads"; the third step shown in Figure 4.8.4. You can skip this step for now, and revisit it later should you wish to experiment with Facebook Paid Marketing.

i) Facebook then takes you to your new Page and will begin to walk you through some options such as Liking your Page and composing your first post. My suggestion is, before you do this, at the very least add a Cover photograph.

To do so, click the "Add a Cover" button and upload a photograph that is striking and appealing to viewers. (Take note of the necessary dimensions of the Cover photograph).

Figure 4.8.5. Adding a Facebook "Cover" image.

j)   Next, click on the "About" button shown below.

Figure 4.8.6. Facebook's "About" button to add information.

k)   This will lead you to the Information Page that you completed earlier, only now, when you hover over the Information section with your mouse, it brings up the two "Edit" links on the right-hand side. This enables you to add more content, thereby enhancing your ranking - *do it!*

Figure 4.8.7. Facebook's "Edit" buttons to add further content.

l) Click either of the "Edit" links and then add more information and keywords into the description sections. *Don't hold back here!*

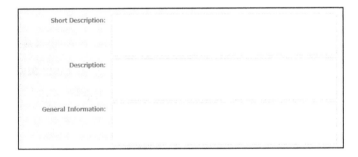

Figure 4.8.8. Facebook's description type boxes.

m) Now that your page is branded and offers an informative overview of your property, begin posting. I recommend sharing a few posts before you invite anyone to Like your Page.

n) To gain Facebook fans, the first step is to Like the Page yourself. To do this, click on the "Like" button that sits to the left of your settings icon beneath your Cover photograph.

Figure 4.8.9. The "Like" button on Facebook.

Once clicked, the button will say "Liked".

o) You are then ready to begin inviting others to Like you Page. This can be done in two ways. The first is by the inviting people you are already personally connected to on Facebook to Like your Page. The second option is to invite email contacts.

Facebook makes it very easy to do both. Simply click on the "Build Audience" button at the top of your Page and then select "Invite Friends..." from the dropdown bar.

Figure 4.8.10. Facebook's "Build Audience" section.

A pop-up will open, showing you thumbnails of all your contacts, divided into two categories: "Recent Interactions" and "Search all friends," as shown in Figure 4.8.11.

Figure 4.8.11. Search for existing contacts on Facebook.

Click on "Search all friends" to view a complete list of your own Facebook connections. Scroll through the list and invite people to Like your Page by simply clicking the checkbox next to their thumbnail. Once you have checked off everyone you wish to invite, click the "Submit" button and Facebook will send your connections the request.

The second option of inviting your email contacts can be performed just as easily by clicking the "Invite Email Contacts…" in the same dropdown bar shown in Figure 4.8.10. Then follow the instructions to send an email to your contacts.

This second option should not be ignored. You likely have staff that you are not personally connected to on Facebook. This option allows you to email all your staff and alert them about the property's new Page. Remember, the more Like's your Page has, the more reach your Page gets!

That's one down. Now let's move on to Twitter.

Step 9: Getting Started on Twitter

Allow 20 – 40 minutes to complete this section.

a) Visit **twitter.com**.

b) Fill in the "New to Twitter" section, regardless of whether you already have a personal account or not. This will allow you to set up a Twitter account specific to your property.

Figure 4.9.1. Twitter's sign in or sign up type boxes.

c) Twitter will recap the information you entered and will ask you to accept their Terms and Conditions before proceeding by clicking "Create my account".

Figure 4.9.2. Twitter's "Create my account" button.

d) You will then be walked through a short tutorial on what a Tweet looks like and how to Follow others.

Figure 4.9.3. Twitter's example of what a Tweet looks like.

Figure 4.9.4. Twitter's example of how to gain followers.

e) *Always choose followers wisely.* Keep in mind that who you choose to follow says a lot about your property. Base your follower selection on industry connection so that your followers are likely to share knowledge that will interest both you and your future followers.

Once you have selected 5 people to follow you will be prompted to click "Next" to proceed.

Figure 4.9.5. Building you Twitter "timeline".

f) The next screen shows you how to search for people in your industry. This will allow you to build a community centered on follows who share your interests and possibly your audience.

In the example below, I typed in the search term "Travel". Travel guides and airlines are excellent choices to follow as they share a common hospitality theme and are likely to already have a following that enjoys travelling and whom are always on the lookout for their next destination. The next destination that could very well be your property!

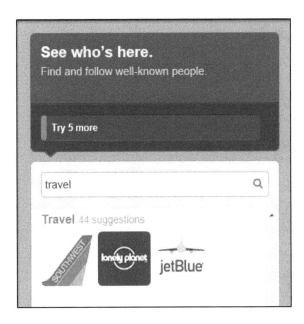

Figure 4.9.6. Finding Twitter profiles to follow.

g) If you click on the Lonely Planet icon shown in Figure 4.9.6. for example, you will be shown suggestions of people to follow who already follow Lonely Planet.

Those that Twitter suggests have a high Klout score (follower to engagement ratio) and are excellent choices to follow and to watch closely in order see what these top Twitter profiles are doing to earn and maintain their viewership.

Click the "Follow" button to become a follower of their Twitter profile.

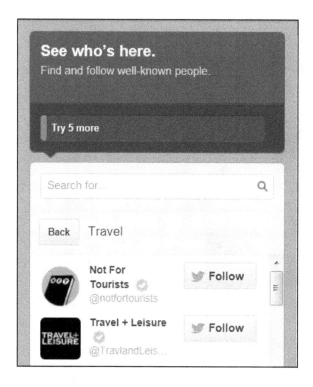

Figure 4.9.7. How to "Follow" someone on Twitter.

h) After selecting 5 additional people to follow based on the keywords you entered, you will again be prompted to click "Next".

Figure 4.9.8. Finding existing contacts on Twitter.

i) You will then be asked to find more contacts securely by logging in to your email accounts. Twitter will help by showing you which of your email contacts are already on Twitter and whom you may want to Follow.

Figure 4.9.9. Search for contacts on Twitter by email.

j) You can also find people by name directly on Twitter by typing a name in the search box, as shown in the example below.

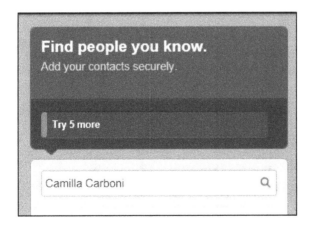

Figure 4.9.10. Searching for contacts on Twitter by name.

k) Scroll through the search results screen to see if you can locate the person you are looking for. If you locate them, click "Follow" and you will begin to receive their Tweets in your Twitter timeline.

Figure 4.9.11. Twitter's example of how to "Follow" a contact.

l) Once you have followed another 5 people, the "Next" button will reappear. Click it and you will be prompted to the first personalization screen, where you can upload a Profile photograph and type in a short description or "Bio" about your property.

As with the Facebook personalization process, do not skip this step. Ensure that both the photograph and description you choose are effective and meaningful. Perhaps you want to place your company logo in the photo spot, or maybe an enticing picture of your property. Whatever you decide on, ensure that it fits with the branding you have chosen. Don't forget to include key search terms in the "Bio" section!

Figure 4.9.12. Twitter's personalization options.

m) Twitter will let you know that your profile setup is complete and will ask you to verify your email address. I personally feel that you have to take a few more steps in branding your account before you actually have a complete profile.

To do this, click on the Settings icon shown below which is always visible on the top right navigation bar of your Twitter profile screen and then select "Settings" from the drop down list.

Figure 4.9.13. The "Settings" button on Twitter.

n) Under "Settings" there are a number of personalization options you may want to utilize. The two most important sections are "Profile" and "Design".

Let's start with the first. Click on the "Profile" button in the list on the left of the screen.

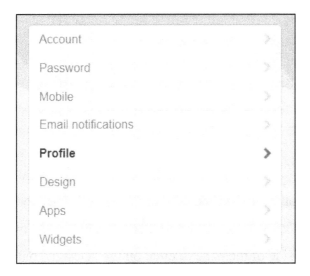

Figure 4.9.14. The "Profile" button on Twitter.

o) On the right hand side of your page the "Profile" options will appear. First upload a "Header" image to extend the branding of your profile. You can think of this as Twitter's equivalent to Facebook's Cover image.

To upload a Header Image, click "Change header" and follow the prompts.

Figure 4.9.15. Changing the "Header" image on Twitter.

p) Next, add your location and website URL in the appropriate boxes.

Location	
	Where in the world are you?
Website	http://
	Have a homepage or a blog? Put the address here.

Figure 4.9.16. Adding information to your Twitter Profile.

q) Once you have finished editing the "Profile" section, click "Save Changes" on the bottom of the screen and hover back to the left side of the page to click on the "Design" button.

Figure 4.9.17. The "Design" button on Twitter.

r) You will then be shown two options: 1. you can select a premade background, or 2. you can upload your own background. I would strongly suggest the latter in order to add another touch of branding to your Twitter profile.

A beautiful photograph of your property, or even your main attraction, is a perfect choice for the background image. To add your own background image, simply click on the "Change background" button and follow the prompts.

Figure 4.9.18. Twitter's background options.

s) Click "Save changes" once you have completed this step and you are now well on your way to a well-branded Twitter profile. All that is left to do is begin Tweeting and engaging with your potential customers.

Step 10: Firing Up Flickr

Allow 20 – 40 minutes to complete this section.

a) Visit **flickr.com**.

b) Click the "Sign Up" button on the top navigation bar.

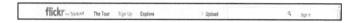

Figure 4.10.1. Signing up for a Flickr account.

c) Flickr will ask if you are a new user or wish to Sign In. In our
case of setting up a new profile, you would select "Create New
Account".

Figure 4.10.2. The "Create New Account" button on Flickr.

d) You will be prompted to create a Yahoo ID. Fill in the steps and then click "Create my account".

Note: Unlike Facebook and Twitter who ask you to check a box stating that you agree to the Terms of Use, Flickr assumes that you agree with their Terms if you click "Create my account" and proceed with the setup process.

Figure 4.10.3. Accepting Flickr's Terms.

e) You will then be asked to set security questions. Complete this step and then click "Done" to proceed to a screen that recaps your information. Review it and click "Get Started".

f) The next step is to choose your Flickr screen name. I know it's tempting to get creative but for purposes of recognition, keep your screen name the name of your property.

Figure 4.10.4. Choosing your Flickr "screen name".

g) If your name happens to already be taken, Flickr will make suggestions for you that may include abbreviating part of the name or adding a character to it. You don't have to settle for one of Flickr's suggestions, you can continue to type in alternatives until you find a name that you like that is available. Remember that your screen name should be identifiable. Once you have your screen name picked out, click "CREATE MY ACCOUNT".

Figure 4.10.5. When your chosen Flickr name is not available.

h) Now the personalization stage begins and here you can unleash your creative spirit (while still keeping on brand of course). Flickr will provide you with three steps to get started.

Figure 4.10.6. Personalizing your Flickr profile.

i) Follow the first step by selecting "Personalize your profile," which leads you to a screen with three sub-steps; "Create you buddy icon," "Choose your custom Flickr URL" and "Personalize your profile".

Figure 4.10.7. Basic Flickr profile enhancements.

j) Click "LET"S DO IT!" and Flickr will walk you through the process. (*I hope you're as excited as Flickr always seems to be!*)

You will first be guided to upload a Profile photograph, which is what Flickr calls a "Buddy Icon". Don't skip this step even though they provide you with an option to do so. Branding your social media pages is a critical part of establishing your online marketing identity.

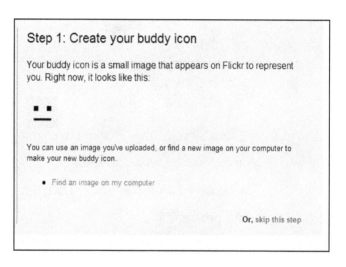

Figure 4.10.8. Creating your "Buddy Icon" on Flickr.

k) Once you have uploaded your "Buddy Icon" image, keep the momentum and move straight on to choosing your Flickr page URL. If possible, I would suggest keeping this the same as the Flickr screen name you chose earlier in the process.

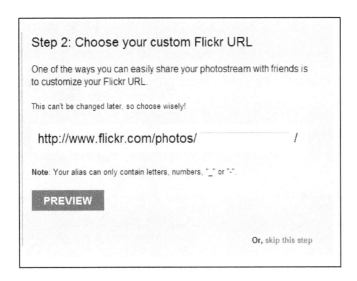

Figure 4.10.9. Choosing your Flickr URL.

l) The last step in this section provides you with the option to add information. I'm sure by now you already know that options to enhance your profile are always a great decision, so write a concise, descriptive and keyword rich overview of your property in the "Description" box as you did with your Facebook and Twitter accounts.

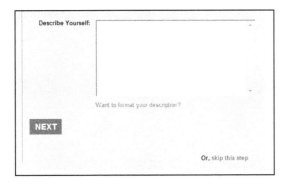

Figure 4.10.10. The descriptive type box on Flickr.

m) Once you have completed this section, Flickr provides you with another upbeat message and asks what you would like to do next. Click "your home page" so that you can immediately proceed with adding color to your profile (*by uploading strategically selected, captivating images of your property of course!*).

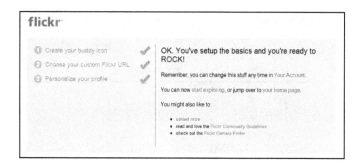

Figure 4.10.11. Returning to your home page to upload images.

n) Flickr allows for a decent number of images to be uploaded. It is certainly great to offer potential customers a large album to click through, but keep in mind that every image you choose to upload should enhance your property's reputation, so choose wisely and favor quality over quantity.

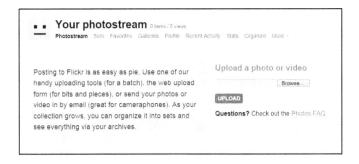

Figure 4.10.12. Uploading images to your Flickr "Photostream".

o) Once you have a number of photographs uploaded, you can organize them into "Sets". This is Flickr's way of helping you stay neat and tidy (*Flickr really is so kind*), and a profile that is easy for your audience to view and navigate.

In the Hotel Industry, you might want to group your images into "Sets" such as Guest Rooms, Gardens, Dining, Activities and Local Attractions.

To do this click on "Organize" in the navigation bar.

Figure 4.10.13. Flickr's "Organize" button to arrange images.

p) The "Batch Organize" screen will appear. Hover your mouse a little to the right and click on the tab next to it that reads "Sets".

Figure 4.10.14. Locating the "Set" button on Flickr.

q) Click on "CREATE YOUR FIRST SET".

Note: once you have created your first Set, this button will read "CREATE NEW SET" in the future.

Figure 4.10.15. Creating a "Set" of images on Flickr.

r) You will then be asked to drag one of your images into the album cover box, title the Set and provide a description, as shown in the screenshot below.

Figure 4.10.16. Adding information to a "Set" on Flickr.

s) That's your cue to stop, drop and drag one of the images from the bottom of your screen into the Set cover box. The "Save" button will now turn blue. Any other images that you would like to group under this Set simply need to dragged and dropped into the large drop-box in the center of the screen. Click "Save" once you have finished adding all the images you would like to this Set.

Figure 4.10.17. Drag and drop images into a "Set" on Flickr.

t) Flickr will then return you to the "Sets" screen where you will now see your magnificent new Set. From here you may click "create a new set" and follow the same steps to group a new set of property images. *Do it now - organization never fails to look impressive!*

Figure 4.10.18. A "Set" on Flickr.

u) When you click on "Photostream" or "Sets" in the navigation bar, you will see how your Sets generate a cleaner look and feel for your Flickr profile.

Figure 4.10.19. A "Set" in your "Photostream" on Flickr.

Step 11: Gearing Up On Pinterest

Allow 20 – 40 minutes to complete this section.

a) Visit **pinterest.com**.

b) Click the "Join Pinterest" button shown below.

Figure 4.11.1. Joining Pinterest.

c) You will be provided with the option to create an account using your email address, Facebook or Twitter. Now that you have all three accounts, you have all the more choices. Click on your pick of the three options and then fill in the required information. Your Username would ideally be the name of your property, because to Pinterest, your Username is your Screen name.

Figure 4.11.2. The first steps in creating a Pinterest account.

d) Before leaving this screen, click on the "Upload your Photo" button on the left and follow the prompts to set up your Profile image. Once this is complete, click on the "Create Account" button on the bottom of the page.

Like Twitter, Pinterest will now help you to become social, by prompting you to "Follow 5 boards".

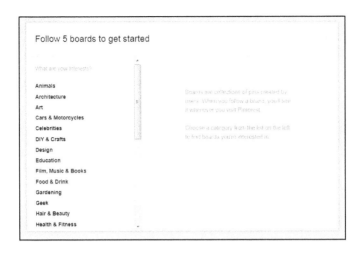

Figure 4.11.3. Following your first 5 "boards" on Pinterest.

e) Using the scroll bar, locate topics that are relevant to your property. If you click on Travel for example, a number of Pinterest boards with popular travel photographs will appear on the right-hand side of the screen as shown in Figure 4.11.4.

Figure 4.11.4. Pinterest shows you how to "Follow" a "board".

f) By moving the scroll bar on the far right, you will find numerous boards related to the topic "Travel," with a "Follow" button beside them. Once you have followed 5 good looking boards, a button will appear on the top right which reads "Next". Click it.

Figure 4.11.5. Finishing the first "Follow" process on Pinterest.

g) You will then land on your newly established Pinterest homepage.

To add your property overview, click on your Username (in this example, "Demonstration") on the top right of the page and select "Settings".

Figure 4.11.6. Adding information to your Pinterest account.

h) Enter any additional information you might like to display, but most importantly, *(I'm sure by now you know what's coming)* write your property overview in the description box, add your address into the location box, and place your website address into the URL box.

Figure 4.11.7. Entering information in your Pinterest account.

i) Once you have completed this step, scroll down and click "Save Profile". This will direct you to your profile page, which will appear rather dull without any imagery (and not at all a true reflection of your property). Begin loading photographs to your page right away by clicking on one of the graphics that read "Create a Board".

Figure 4.11.8. Creating a "Board" on Pinterest.

j) You will then be asked to choose both a name and category for this Board before clicking "Create Board".

Figure 4.11.9. Naming and categorizing a "Board" on Pinterest.

k) Your new Board will now appear on your profile page. Click the "Edit" button on it.

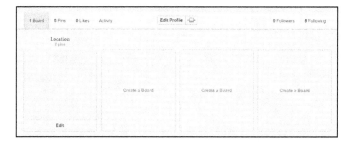

Figure 4.11.10. Editing a Pinterest "Board".

l) Here you can add information about the Board (yet another great place to include keywords). Click "Save Settings" once you are done.

Edit Board / Location		Delete Board
Title	Location	
Description		
Category	Travel ▼	
Who can pin?	Name or email address of a friend...	Invite
	Demonstration Work You created this board	
	Save Settings	

Figure 4.11.11. Adding information to a Pinterest "Board".

m) Pinterest will then show you what your Board summary looks like. (*You guessed it! The information you just entered will appear in place of the text I typed which reads "This is where the overview of your property will be"*).

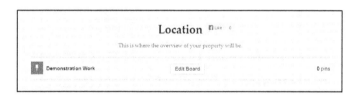

Figure 4.11.12. Example of a Pinterest "Board" Title.

n) Next click on "Add" in the top navigation bar to begin uploading much needed imagery to your new Board.

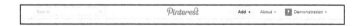

Figure 4.11.13. Adding images to your Pinterest account.

o) Start by selecting "Upload a Pin" and follow the prompts to add images of your property to your Pinterest Page, once again paying close attention to the quality of the images you choose.

My suggestion is to fill four Boards immediately in order to ensure that your Page looks complete and has enough content to engage potential consumers, as demonstrated in Figure 4.11.14.

Figure 4.11.14. Example of four completed Pinterest "Boards".

As you post images to both Facebook and Twitter, as part of your Social Calendar (which we'll get to in Chapter Five: Step 16), and start finding user photography of your property and destination on Flickr (which we'll address in Chapter Six: Step 19), you can Pin all of those to your Pinterest Page. That's my tip to keeping your Pinterest account active, by continuing to add fresh content for your online audience, with little to no additional work.

Step 12: Managing Your TripAdvisor Listing

Allow 15 – 25 minutes to complete this section.

a) Visit **tripadvisor.com**.

b) Search for your property's name in the search box on the top right of the navigation bar.

Figure 4.12.1. Searching for your property on TripAdvisor.

c) A dropdown list will appear as you type and somewhere in it you should find your property's name. In the screenshot below, I demonstrate this by typing the word "Test".

Figure 4.12.2. TripAdvisor search example.

If you cannot locate your property, you will need to visit http://www.tripadvisor.com/pages/getlisted_hotel.html and follow the instructions to set up a listing before you can proceed with the next steps.

d) Click on your property's name and you will be taken to your property's listing page on TripAdvisor.

This is a prime example of an audience already talking about your property, whether you have been aware of it or not.

Scroll down this page and you will find a section addressing you, the rightful "Owner" who, thankfully, has the right to claim and manage the listing (*to a certain extent at least*).

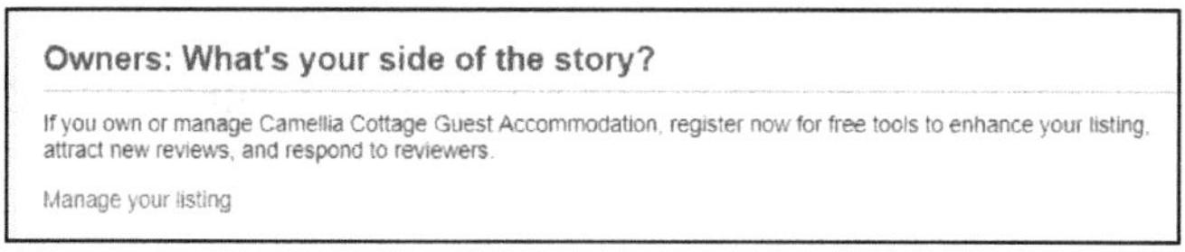

Owners: What's your side of the story?

If you own or manage Camellia Cottage Guest Accommodation, register now for free tools to enhance your listing, attract new reviews, and respond to reviewers.

Manage your listing

Figure 4.12.3. The "Manage your listing" link on TripAdvisor.

e) Click on the "Manage your listing" link shown at the bottom of the above screenshot and the Management Center page will open, asking if you are in fact affiliated with the property. Click on the "Register now" button to get started.

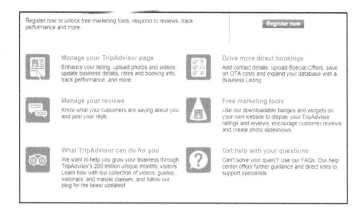

Figure 4.12.4. TripAdvisor's "Register now" button.

f) If you are not signed in to TripAdvisor, a pop-up will ask you to sign in using either your Facebook or email account. If you are not already a member, it's time to join the world of budding travel writers and sign up now. Like Facebook, you require a personal TripAdvisor account in order to Manage a Listing.

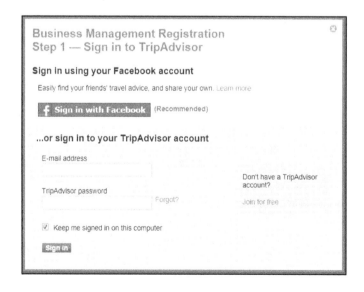

Figure 4.12.5. The sign-up options for a TripAdvisor account.

g) You will then be required to complete and submit information in order for TripAdvisor to verify that you are indeed a legal representative of the property. Click "Continue" to begin this process.

Figure 4.12.6. TripAdvisor's "Listing" Manager tools.

h) Fill in the information as requested and then at the bottom of the pop-up box you will need to check that you agree to the Terms before clicking "Continue".

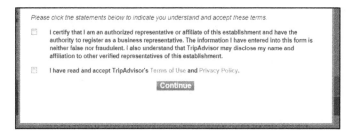

Figure 4.12.7. Agreeing to TripAdvisor's Terms.

i) The last step is to provide evidence or legal documents as proof that you are authorized to Manage the Listing.

You have three options to choose from: 1. show TripAdvisor that you manage this property on Facebook, 2. provide a credit card, or 3. send documentation such as an electricity bill that includes your property name. Since you should now have your Facebook property Page set up and rolling, this would be the easiest option.

Figure 4.12.8. Verification to Manage a TripAdvisor "Listing".

j) Once you have completed this step, you will have access to the TripAdvisor Management Center. Browse through what is available to you by clicking on each section header shown below.

Figure 4.12.9. TripAdvisor's "Management Center".

k) Once you are familiar with everything available to you, you probably want to keep things simple and just use the "Quick Links" box on future visits. This box sits on the top right corner of the Management Center page.

Figure 4.12.10. TripAdvisor's "Quick Links" navigation.

l) All four "Quick Links" are very useful and I encourage you to use them all, regularly. Most importantly, you should become very familiar with the first one, "Write a management response" and we will cover this in detail in Chapter Six: Step 20.

You should now have all your Pages set up and well branded. Give yourself a pat on the back. You are officially ready for social engagement!

Chapter Five:

Tell It, Share It, Picture It

Going social can be both daunting and exciting, but it should only be the latter. Once you are familiar with the industry tricks and best practices, you will be creating content and posting away in no time at all.

This Chapter walks you through the steps of creating good content and shares how best to deliver it to your audience.

These steps feature:

- **Choose Your Content Wisely** – cater to your audience
- **Be Both Factual And Fun** – keep it interesting
- **Never Say "I"** – don't alienate your audience
- **Build Your Social Calendar** – get organized
- **Scheduling Options** – make your life easy

Step 13: Choose Your Content Wisely

We know from Step 1: *Understand Your Audience* that an audience consists of individuals with subjective outlooks and preferences. Therefore, to attract and sustain a large audience, you must cater to the middle ground, or stereotypical member of your audience group. This same rule applies when it comes to content.

You want to share content that appeals to your generalized audience profile and then offer a few further reaching topics to pique the interest of individuals.

As with any large group or audience, there exists a law of averages that can be illustrated by a normal distribution curve.

It is a scientifically proven phenomenon that has been studied in depth for centuries and can be applied in every instance in which a group of individuals is summarized as a generalized whole.

What the curve illustrates is that, despite the group consisting of individuals who are unique, there always exists a predominant average. This notion is shown between point x and point y on the diagram below:

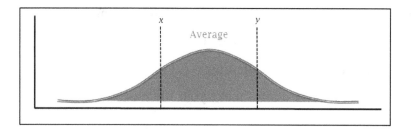

Figure 5.13.1. Normalized distribution curve shows an average.

This majority is what you identified as your target audience mold in Chapter One's profiling exercise that placed your typical audience member into a category, such as Example One's world-traveler-adventure-seeker-fine-dining-enthusiast who enjoys luxury experiences.

Using this particular audience profile as an example, the law of averages might result in the following content ideas being appropriate to this group:

- Outdoor Dining
- Catamaran Cruising
- Skiing
- Spa Treatments
- Local Eateries
- Farmer's Markets
- Museums
- Wineries
- Monuments
- Local Traditions
- Art Galleries

These are things that the generalized audience may want to hear about in your online conversations. They will likely look for such topics in your content and you will therefore need to include such content in order for them to stay interested and involved as fans and followers.

Focus the majority of your content on such conversations and you will have a campaign that caters to your audience based on the law of averages.

"Statistics may be defined as 'a body of methods for making wise decisions in the face of uncertainty.'"

~ W.A. Wallis

However, there still exist the two ends of the curve that have a lesser sum of normalized distribution, but nonetheless still exist in your audience mold. Your campaign will succeed without touching on these two ends, but it will thrive if you do include them.

Not everyone enjoys trying new foods, hiking, bathing in a natural hot spring in the depth of winter, or learning about the history of your property. But, some members of your audience will enjoy those things and, by catering to individualistic desires, you create a more comprehensive experience for your audience members.

Step 14: Be Both Factual and Fun

In choosing your content based on the law of averages, consider tone; making sure that your content is both factual and fun. Unexciting social media pages that are merely fact based and scientific will not capture the attention of a large audience mold. On the other hand, pages that merely focus on lighthearted jokes and sayings, will lose the attention of the learned audience member who desires both enjoyment and stimulation.

I firmly believe that no matter what your product or type of property, a balance between factual and fun content will capture and maintain the greatest attention.

You may want to share an inspiring quote one day, a history fact the next and a fun photograph the day after. Keep in mind that your history fact can still be shared in a light hearted manner, and your fun photograph could be presented in a serious way, or vice versa, as demonstrated in the following examples:

Factual post example

"100 years ago today the President set foot on our marble floors".

Factual post example with image

"Skiing has been a recreational activity since 1861".

Figure 5.14.1. Factual post example using a skiing image.

Lighthearted post example

"The next time you set foot on our shiny marble floors, know that you have walked in the path of an icon - the President visited us over a decade ago today!"

Lighthearted post example with image

"We love skiing! Our favorite thing is taking in the winter wonderland scenery from our guestroom balconies. What is your favorite thing about ski season?

Figure 5.14.2. Lighthearted post example with the skiing image.

The same subject matter can be delivered in very different styles and tones. Mix things up and make it interesting for your audience.

Step 15: Never Say "I"

There are people who will disagree with me on this (and you must ultimately do what you feel is best for your audience), but I firmly believe that all online content, including comments, posts and tweets should not include the word "I"; with the exception of cases where you are the product itself, for example a chef or an actor.

This is more effective because your brand is an entity and should be presented as such. Even if you are the CEO or the Content Manager and are writing all the online copy, stating "I can offer you a world class experience that you don't want to miss" is less powerful than "(Your Property Name) offers a world class experience not to be missed".

The biggest use of "I" often manifests itself in social media posts and breaks a brands' dream-like illusion because it reduces it to a person rather than a product. Below are a few examples of what I mean by this:

Post example using "I"

"I took this picture; let me know what you think?"

Comment Response example using "I"

"I am so pleased you like the photograph."

Tweet example using "I"

"I'm going to experience our dinner this evening under the stars."

When "I" is used the audience is isolated from the action; they are now merely looking in at what the person in charge of the property's social media is doing and saying. The audience feels like they are talking to an individual, not the property.

I know what you're probably thinking here, "but in this technological world it's nice to speak with an individual" and I absolutely agree that when it comes to calling customer service or submitting a message or email request, it is best to reach an individual. However, when your property is represented online, it should be kept as an inclusive experience and not reduced to one person's experience with it.

What if those same three examples were rephrased like this?:

Post example without using "I"

"Today in Cabo San Lucas ~ isn't it gorgeous?"

Comment Response example without using "I"

"We are delighted that you enjoyed the photograph."

Tweet example without using "I"

"Experience dinner under the stars."

By not using "I" you are commenting as the property, not as an individual.

Your audience is no longer an outsider looking in at what you, as the "I" may be doing, instead they envision themselves doing the things you are posting about. Suddenly your audience feels a part of your day-to-day offerings and a natural progression occurs: from voyeur to desire to guest.

Step 16: Build Your Social Calendar

Calendars serve a great purpose in keeping you organized, on track and on time. They provide an overview of your upcoming month, what you have planned, on which days and at what hour. Calendars, be they on your wall or on your phone, should be your best friend. A Social Calendar is no different. It lets you plan, day by day, hour by hour, your schedule for the duration of the month. Only in the case of the Social Calendar, it's not what you're going to do each day, but what you're going to share, post, tweet, etc.

It is worthwhile to take the time to create a social calendar, which can be done as partially or comprehensively as you desire. This process will help you to ensure that you cover the topics you selected in Step 13, in order to effectively market to your audience. Social Calendar creation covers the following steps:

- Event and Holiday Placement
- Generalized Topic Selection
- Individualistic Topic Selection
- Tone Selection
- Content Creation
- Time Stamp Insertion (optional)

To start, begin with a blank calendar (get yours at camillacarboni.com) and start by notating any specific events or holidays that you may wish to include in your content under Step 1.

Tip: Search the internet for food celebrations, events, famous dates and birthdays etc., to help you come up with ideas to formulate your posts.

Calendar Worksheet One

Month:	April	Year:	2013			
Monday 1	Tuesday 2	Wednesday 3	Thursday 4	Friday 5	Saturday 6	Sunday 7
						World Health Day

Step 1 / Step 2 / Step 3 / Step 4 / Step 5

Monday 8	Tuesday 9	Wednesday 10	Thursday 11	Friday 12	Saturday 13	Sunday 14
			Fondue Day			

Step 1 / Step 2 / Step 3 / Step 4 / Step 5

Monday 15	Tuesday 16	Wednesday 17	Thursday 18	Friday 19	Saturday 20	Sunday 21

Step 1 / Step 2 / Step 3 / Step 4 / Step 5

Monday 22	Tuesday 23	Wednesday 24	Thursday 25	Friday 26	Saturday 27	Sunday 28
Earth Day					Prime Rib Day	

Step 1 / Step 2 / Step 3 / Step 4 / Step 5

Monday 29	Tuesday 30					

Step 1 / Step 2 / Step 3 / Step 4 / Step 5

Figure 5.16.1. Social Calendar Worksheet One.

The second step is to think of generalized topics that fit into your "average curve" and place them in the majority of dates on your calendar under Step 2. Figure 5.16.2. provides an example of this using the list created in Chapter Five: Step 13:

Calendar Worksheet Two

Month: April   Year: 2013

	Monday 1	Tuesday 2	Wednesday 3	Thursday 4	Friday 5	Saturday 6	Sunday 7
Step 1							World Health Day
Step 2	Spa Treatments		Local Eateries		Skiing	Wineries	
Step 3							
Step 4							
Step 5							

	Monday 8	Tuesday 9	Wednesday 10	Thursday 11	Friday 12	Saturday 13	Sunday 14
Step 1				Fondue Day			
Step 2	Fine Wine	Customs				Outdoor Dining	Museums
Step 3							
Step 4							
Step 5							

	Monday 15	Tuesday 16	Wednesday 17	Thursday 18	Friday 19	Saturday 20	Sunday 21
Step 1							
Step 2			Skiing		Wineries		Customs
Step 3							
Step 4							
Step 5							

	Monday 22	Tuesday 23	Wednesday 24	Thursday 25	Friday 26	Saturday 27	Sunday 28
Step 1	Earth Day					Prime Rib Day	
Step 2		Monuments	Outdoor Dining		Art Galleries		
Step 3							
Step 4							
Step 5							

	Monday 29	Tuesday 30					
Step 1							
Step 2	Property Info.	Local Eateries					
Step 3							
Step 4							
Step 5							

Figure 5.16.2. Social Calendar Worksheet Two.

Now that you have taken care of the generalized topics, you need to address the ends of the curve where content will be more specified. On your calendar, under Step 3, mark placeholders for individualistic content in the remainder of the spaces (this should not exceed 10 to 15 percent of the posts on your social calendar).

Calendar Worksheet Three

Month: April Year: 2013

	Monday 1	Tuesday 2	Wednesday 3	Thursday 4	Friday 5	Saturday 6	Sunday 7
Step 1							World Health Day
Step 2	Spa Treatments		Local Eateries		Skiing	Wineries	
Step 3		Quote					
Step 4							
Step 5							

	Monday 8	Tuesday 9	Wednesday 10	Thursday 11	Friday 12	Saturday 13	Sunday 14
Step 1				Fondue Day			
Step 2	Fine Wine	Customs				Outdoor Dining	Museums
Step 3					History		
Step 4							
Step 5							

	Monday 15	Tuesday 16	Wednesday 17	Thursday 18	Friday 19	Saturday 20	Sunday 21
Step 1							
Step 2			Skiing		Wineries		Customs
Step 3		Local Saying				Onsite Activity	
Step 4							
Step 5							

	Monday 22	Tuesday 23	Wednesday 24	Thursday 25	Friday 26	Saturday 27	Sunday 28
Step 1	Earth Day					Prime Rib Day	
Step 2		Monuments	Outdoor Dining		Art Galleries		
Step 3							Fact
Step 4							
Step 5							

	Monday 29	Tuesday 30					
Step 1							
Step 2	Property Info.	Local Eateries					
Step 3							
Step 4							
Step 5							

Figure 5.16.3. Social Calendar Worksheet Three.

The fourth step is to determine how you wish to formulate the topics on your calendar in terms of tone. Think about which topics could be factual and which could be fun.

Note: You can share a fact in a lighthearted way and you can take a dry approach to a joke. This step simply serves to remind you to consider tone when crafting your subject matter.

Proceed now with filling in your choice of tone on your calendar under Step 4.

Calendar Worksheet Four

| Month: | April | Year: | 2013 |

	Monday 1	Tuesday 2	Wednesday 3	Thursday 4	Friday 5	Saturday 6	Sunday 7
Step 1							World Health Day
Step 2	Spa Treatments		Local Eateries		Skiing	Wineries	
Step 3		Quote					
Step 4	Lighthearted	Factual	Lighthearted		Lighthearted	Lighthearted	Factual
Step 5							

	Monday 8	Tuesday 9	Wednesday 10	Thursday 11	Friday 12	Saturday 13	Sunday 14
Step 1				Fondue Day			
Step 2	Fine Wine	Customs				Outdoor Dining	Museums
Step 3					History		
Step 4	Lighthearted	Lighthearted		Factual	Factual	Lighthearted	Factual
Step 5							

	Monday 15	Tuesday 16	Wednesday 17	Thursday 18	Friday 19	Saturday 20	Sunday 21
Step 1							
Step 2			Skiing		Wineries		Customs
Step 3		Local Saying				Onsite Activity	
Step 4		Lighthearted	Lighthearted		Factual	Lighthearted	Factual
Step 5							

	Monday 22	Tuesday 23	Wednesday 24	Thursday 25	Friday 26	Saturday 27	Sunday 28
Step 1	Earth Day					Prime Rib Day	
Step 2		Monuments	Outdoor Dining		Art Galleries		
Step 3							Fact
Step 4	Lighthearted	Factual	Lighthearted		Factual	Lighthearted	Lighthearted
Step 5							

	Monday 29	Tuesday 30					
Step 1							
Step 2	Property Info.	Local Eateries					
Step 3							
Step 4	Factual	Lighthearted					
Step 5							

Figure 5.16.4. Social Calendar Worksheet Four.

If you prefer to plan more freely, put your feet up and stop the process right here. You can simply decide daily or perhaps weekly what your actual content looks like, based on this high-level calendar.

If however, you like the idea of having pre-planned content (you may even wish to pre-schedule your posts and I'll talk more about that in the next Chapter), let's buckle down a little longer and complete the remaining two steps of the Social Calendar.

This is where it gets exciting! This is when you finally begin to compile the actual content.

The limited space on the calendar forces you to keep you content concise, which is a proven best practice in social media. Using captivating imagery is another excellent tip that attracts viewership. You may want to make a note on the calendar of a particular photograph name you wish to incorporate.

Go through each day on your calendar and formulate your content using the topics and style you have decided upon, as shown below.

Calendar Worksheet Five

Month:	April	Year:	2024

	Monday 1	Tuesday 2	Wednesday 3	Thursday 4	Friday 5	Saturday 6	Sunday 7
Step 1							World Health Day
Step 2	Spa Treatments		Local Eateries		Skiing	Wineries	
Step 3		Quote					
Step 4	Lighthearted	Factual	Lighthearted		Lighthearted	Lighthearted	Factual
Step 5	Beat the Monday blues and relax with us (pic)	"You get educated by travelling" ~ Solange Knowles	Our locals know how to cook! (pic & restaurant link)		The sunshine is hitting the slopes. Are you? (pic)	A great day for wine tasting: (link to wine tour)	Look inward for "The greatest wealth is health" ~ Virgil

	Monday 8	Tuesday 9	Wednesday 10	Thursday 11	Friday 12	Saturday 13	Sunday 14
Step 1				Fondue Day			
Step 2	Fine Wine	Customs				Outdoor Dining	Museums
Step 3					History		
Step 4	Lighthearted	Lighthearted		Factual	Factual	Lighthearted	Factual
Step 5	"Wine is bottled poetry" - Robert Louis Stevenson (winetasting pic)	Colorodeo?! The first rodeo on record was at Deer Trail on July 4, 1869.		First served in 1699, the fondue returns with local cheeses (pic)	Did you know that the entry hall used to be the parlor?	Picnic season has arrived...we'll pack, you picnic! (pic)	Our town museum boasts skis from the 1890's.

	Monday 15	Tuesday 16	Wednesday 17	Thursday 18	Friday 19	Saturday 20	Sunday 21
Step 1							
Step 2			Skiing		Wineries		Customs
Step 3		Local Saying				Onsite Activity	
Step 4		Lighthearted	Lighthearted		Factual	Lighthearted	Factual
Step 5		Ever heard of Red Snow? They say it's the result of a single-celled plant!	For just two poles and two giant feet this sport really took on!		Colorado is home to over 100 wineries. Cheers to that! (pic)	We salute to over 300 days of sun a year. Join us daily at 8am. (yoga pic)	There were once 5 dialects of Arapaho. Less than 500 men still speak it today.

	Monday 22	Tuesday 23	Wednesday 24	Thursday 25	Friday 26	Saturday 27	Sunday 28
Step 1	Earth Day					Prime Rib Day	
Step 2		Monuments	Outdoor Dining		Art Galleries		
Step 3							Fact
Step 4	Lighthearted	Factual	Lighthearted		Factual	Lighthearted	Lighthearted
Step 5	"The earth laughs in flowers" - R. W. Emerson Happy Earth Day!	Did you know: 3 U.S. Navy warships have been named USS Colorado? (pic)	Escape the dining room and take a sleigh ride to a dinner cabin (pic)		The valley is home to 50 local artists and over 20 original galleries (pic)	Awaken your taste buds: It's Prime Rib Day & we're cooking! (pic)	Can you believe Denver's first liquor license was only issued in the 1860s.

	Monday 29	Tuesday 30
Step 1		
Step 2	Property Info.	Local Eateries
Step 3		
Step 4	Factual	Lighthearted
Step 5	When work calls, we answer; when relaxation calls, we indulge. (pic)	Hungry? After a day of skiing you have a great excuse to eat dessert! (pic)

Figure 5.16.5. Social Calendar Worksheet Five.

Once the fifth step is complete, you may consider taking it to the advanced level of social calendar creation and, using your Insights analysis as a guide (to be covered in Chapter Six: Step 18), determine the time of day that you feel would best suit these posts and gain the greatest reach.

To remind yourself you could simply place a time stamp above each post on the calendar.

Please note, however, that you should never post consistently at one specific time. Social media must be social to succeed, so your content must appear natural and thoughtful, never contrived and computerized.

I'm going to repeat that – it's important! **Social media must be social to succeed.**

> "Focus on how to be social,
> not how to do social"
>
> ~ Jay Baer

That's your queue to start engaging (*and never stop!*)

Step 17: Scheduling Options

Once you have your social calendar prepared, you may choose to post your content directly to your social networks at the time you have chosen each day as a manual task, or you could schedule the posts in advance and have them post automatically to your social networking sites.

If you prefer the second option, there are numerous tools available that can assist you with pre-scheduling content. It's really just a matter of personal preference and finding the tool that works best for you. You may want to start looking at popular options by visiting SocialOomph, HootSuite and TweetDeck.

SocialOomph – socialoomph.com

For the literal thinker; SocialOomph is straightforward and systematic. It is a great tool for simple scheduling.

HootSuite – hootsuite.com

For the lateral thinker; HootSuite offers a dashboard that provides a holistic overview of your social media channels. Like SocialOomph, it is an entirely web-based tool and also allows for easy scheduling. HootSuite has a channel limit; however, if you decide this is the tool for you, you may choose to upgrade at a nominal fee and obtain the glorified freedom of unlimited channel usage.

TweetDeck – tweetdeck.com

Also for the lateral thinker, TweetDeck offers a dashboard view of your Tweets in real time. Unlike HootSuite and SocialOomph, TweetDeck requires a download in order to run. The great thing about TweetDeck is it updates your data in real time, rather than pulling content every few minutes. It also allows for unlimited channels. The bad news is that TweetDeck no longer supports Facebook, so if you are looking for tool to manage all of your social networks, this is not your answer.

All three tools are currently free (for the basic version), so experiment with them and find out which one works best for you. *Don't be shy, be social!*

Chapter Six:

Industry Essentials

You could stop here, but you shouldn't. While good content plays a large role in the success of a social media campaign, there are a number of insider tips that will move you from good to great.

Now is the time to start learning how to maximize your reach – to work smarter, not harder – by means of the following steps:

- **Learn From Your Insights** – use data to your advantage
- **Cash In On Free Exposure** – learn to leverage reach
- **Pay Attention to TripAdvisor** – listen and respond
- **Spread The Love** – be humble and likeable

Step 18: Learn From Your Insights

Once you are set up and actively posting, commenting and tweeting in your brand voice, it's time to take a look at your Insights. Facebook offers a fantastic free tool that captures data and statistics that you can and should be using to your benefit. To access your Page Insights, click on the "See All" link on the top right of the "Insights" widget that will appear when you log in to your Page, as shown in Figure 6.18.1.

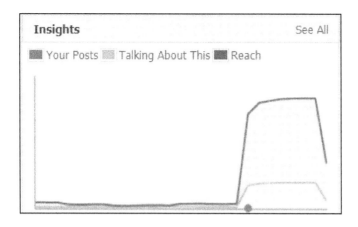

Figure 6.18.1. Facebook's "Insights" widget.

<u>Note:</u> Your Page must have 30 Likes before Facebook will grant you access to the Insights tool. Refer back to Chapter Four: Step 8: point o) for directions on how to increase your fan count by way of your personal connections.

There are three key elements you should pay close attention to when using the Insights tool:

- Geographical breakdown
- Gender breakdown
- Readership count

Let's delve in to each element separately.

Geographical breakdown

Geographical breakdown is important because it tells you these fundamental things:

- Where the majority of your audience resides
- If you are appealing to a widespread locale (statewide, national, international)
- What is the best time of day to post

Gender Breakdown

Gender breakdown is interesting because it can provide you with insight into potentially favorable subject matter. If you find that your page has a significantly larger male following than female following, then you might want to think about incorporating typical male interests into your posts. For example, perhaps you have a great bar on property that airs every football game, or you offer beer tastings, or you have a weekly gentleman's golf challenge. You could then post about these offerings to appeal to your male followers. The key is to always focus on things that the majority of your audience might like.

On the other hand, if you have a predominantly female following, the exclusive gentleman's golf post idea would likely not be very successful. Instead you might want to focus on a spa treatment or a specialty cocktail at sunset.

It does happen in some cases (though I have not seen it very often) that the gender breakdown is almost equal. In this case you should keep your posts gender neutral for the most part and experiment with a few gender specific examples now and then, keeping a close watch on your Readership Count Insights to see how such posts are responded to.

Readership Count

The last of the top three most useful Facebook Insights is Readership Count. It quite possibly offers the most beneficial data as it provides you with an overview of which posts are receiving the greatest viewership or reach.

Take a close look at your best performing posts over the last two weeks and see if you can identify any patterns. Consider the following questions to help you analyze possible trends:

- Did those posts incorporate an image?
- Were they posted at a certain time of day?
- Did they have a similar subject matter?
- Did they share a tone?
- Were they statements or questions?

Analyze the information carefully. Act on it immediately.

Begin trying a few different things in your posts based on assumptions you have made from analyzing your Insights, and then watch closely and see what works and what doesn't.

I can't stress this enough that an effective campaign caters to it's audience and constantly redefines itself based on what the audience shows that they want. Keep a close eye on the Insights tool and adapt to what your audience is telling you. Rinse and repeat.

Step 19: Cash In On Free Exposure

You have no doubt heard of the phrase, "work smarter...not harder". It was coined by Allan F. Mogensen in the 1930's and remains just as relevant today, especially in our inundated technological world. You can utilize this philosophy very effectively in social media marketing. By working smart, your efforts can be magnified enormously through clever leverage of social reach.

My favorite example of this is Flickr; a tool that is underappreciated and in many cases ignored as a social networking tactic. Here me out: Flickr, while originally a photo storage platform, offers the ability to both add your own imagery and, most importantly, to add other's imagery to your own album.

If you have a tool such as ReviewAnalyst, finding images related to your property is very easy. If not, you'll need to spend some time searching for your property's name on Flickr. You may also want to search for locations or attractions in your area that could be relevant to your portfolio of images.

You can do this by logging in to your Flickr account and performing a search. If your property is located in Aspen for example, you could perform a search such as the one shown below.

Figure 6.19.1. Searching for photographs on Flickr.

A search of "Aspen accommodation" returns numerous pages of imagery. You would then scroll through the results and identify photographs of your property, or even an attraction or landmark in the area that may appeal to your audience as a possible experience to partake in while they visit your property. When you click on a photograph icon, the image will enlarge.

The next step is where it really gets tough. Just kidding, it really could not be easier and yet it is so incredibly effective. Simply click on the star at the top left of the photograph you have identified as one you wish to associate with your property, and watch the star turn pink.

Figure 6.19.2. Adding to your "Favorite's" album button on Flickr.

Just like that, in one click of a button, the photograph has been added to *your* favorite's album.

This photograph will now be featured as part of your extended gallery and better yet, it will appear in search results when people surf the internet for images of your property. By using Flickr in this (smart) way, you can create an extensive library of images for your audience to enjoy, without the costs involved with producing or purchasing photography.

The art of leverage can also be easily achieved on both Facebook and Twitter.

Perhaps your property is located next to a popular outlet mall or tourist attraction that has its own Facebook page with thousands of fans. By simply interacting with the fans on such a Facebook page, you gain extended readership and presence in the community.

On Twitter, a simple trick is to use popular hashtags in your tweets. Keep it relevant, so use hashtags that your prospective audience would likely respond to or search for. In the case of hospitalilty, you may want to include the hashtag travel, or perhaps adventure, destination, relaxation or a particular keyword that is popular in your specific location or that describes your property. The following example employs the hashtag Travel.

Figure 6.19.3. Tweeting with a # (hashtag).

Social Media is a fantastic medium that enables you to gain quick and easy presence for your property, if you leverage reach effectively. Try it yourself, and then nurture the newfound connections you make and they will, in turn, want to remain a part of your online community.

Step 20: Pay Attention to TripAdvisor

TripAdvisor is a site that cannot be ignored by anyone in the Hotel Industry. It is arguably more important than a presence on Facebook and Twitter, though I do encourage you to touch as many social bases as you can.

With over 200 million unique visitors per day (according to Google Analytics, worldwide data, March 2013), TripAdvisor has an extensive audience of its own. This audience is no doubt already commenting on your property and using this information to decide if they wish to become a guest or not. You cannot prevent this, nor do you want to. You *must* however manage your listing on the site in order to control the content to the extent that it is possible to do so. If you have not yet done this, refer back to Chapter Four: Step 12 for a guide to claiming ownership of your property, *then listen carefully*:

Reviews, good or bad, are your best friend. They present an opportunity to engage the reviewer – someone who felt passionately enough about their experience at your property to write about it – and they enable you the social real estate on TripAdvisor to share your property's voice with a wider audience.

How? By simply responding! My belief is that you should respond to every single review (*good or bad!*)

Why? A good review was written by a person who has just provided you with some of the best social word of mouth marketing available, and they deserve to be thanked profusely for doing so. A bad review was written by someone who had an unfavorable experience at your property and is sharing what went wrong. They too deserve to be thanked for two reasons: 1. because without constructive criticism you cannot ever discover the weak points of your property and improve them and 2. it's your chance to defend yourself (in a very subtle and respectful way).

On that last point there is a lot to be said about social etiquette and it's no different on TripAdvisor. You will have times when you have to address a difficult subject and you have to do so in a way that lets both the reviewer and the wider audience know that you genuinely care. Let's look at an example of how to approach bad reviews tactfully.

Review Example

"My friend and I were expecting a great vacation – only to find that your hotel didn't even have a room ready for us. We checked in after the daily check in time and were given a key, but when we entered the room it was a complete mess from the last guest. Trash, used towels, the works. What a nice start to our vacation and way to make us feel welcome. Overall our time was fine, but we were left with a bad impression and don't think we'd come back because of it."

Response Example

"Thank you so much for taking the time to share your experience with us. We certainly understand that arriving to find your guestroom unmade must have been a less than pleasing start to your vacation and we sincerely apologize. We pride ourselves in our hospitality and we live to make our guests feel welcome. While this is not a common occurrence, we want to make sure that all measures are taken to ensure this is an isolated instance. We have addressed your experience with all Managers involved with the preparation and allocation of guestrooms and we thank you again for alerting us to this unusual situation so that we could take these steps toward continual improvement. We sincerely hope that you did enjoy our typical high standard of hospitality throughout the remainder of your stay. We extend a warm welcome in the hope that you will visit us again; we would be delighted for the opportunity to deliver our usual exceptional customer service. Many thanks again from all of us."

When you respond to reviews your audience receives both sides of the story. It levels the playing field and, very importantly, lets your audience know that you are listening. It may sound insignificant, but being heard is a basic human need and you would be surprised just how many people have written to thank me over the years for taking the time to merely write back. In my hands on experience managing social media for properties over the last decade, TripAdvisor has consistently shown to have one of the most rewarding social ROIs.

People have shared that they choose to visit the property based on the responses to reviews alone. They have called General Managers and expressed how wonderful it is to see a property actively participating with guests post-stay. They have become avid Facebook fans as a result. People have even sent me gifts and painted me artwork! Trust me, if you do nothing else, please don't ignore TripAdvisor. It is a time consuming task - but trust me – it is well worth the effort.

Step 21: Spread The Love

In social media you must remain humble to succeed. After all, without your fans and followers, you have no audience to interact with and to create-the-dream for. You are present on social media because your customers are – you are entering their turf – the places they frequent online.

Throughout your interactions you must keep this in the back of your mind. Your audience should drive your posts and responses, and you should thank them for their online interaction with your property.

Shout out's, thanks, genuine questions and invited responses always peak and retain audiences' attention. It's just human nature and psychology – we all want to be heard and appreciated – so make your audience feel that way.

"Social Media is about the people!
Not about your business. Provide for the
people & the people will provide for you."

~ Matt Goulart

I believe that:

- **Response is crucial.** When someone takes the time to comment on your page, you must *always* respond.
- **All posts should be valued.** When a customer shares an unfavorable experience, *do not delete the post*. Instead, thank them for sharing it with you and let them know that you never want even one person to have that experience and are working with your management to correct it immediately.
- **Thank You's are in order.** When a customer shares a photograph or a compliment, thank them profusely. Tell them how happy you are to see or hear that they had a wonderful experience at, or while visiting, your property.
- **Your customer should be involved.** Ask your audience for advice and suggestions, maybe for ideas on naming a new drink, or whether they would prefer to see yoga or rafting as a new included activity at your property.
- **Your audience comes first.** Let them know, without a single doubt in their mind, that you are grateful for their participation in your online community and that you wish they would visit again soon.

Chapter Seven:

Concluding Thoughts, Until We Meet Again

As you move through monthly social calendar creations, daily posting and (hopefully hourly) interactions, remember that last crucial point – your audience comes first, always. If you do this, you act with social integrity, you follow up and you genuinely enjoy engaging with your online community by providing them with the information and images they want to see, Social Media Marketing will no longer seem a daunting and overwhelming idea. It's just about representing your property, nicely.

So relax, welcome engagement and have fun with this!

After all, social media is but an extension of everyday interaction. Keep it on brand, but keep it social and you will succeed.

Glossary Of Terms

audience. The people viewing your content.

best practice. A tip or idea that has proven successful.

Board. A display box to upload photographs to on Pinterest.

brand voice. The style and tone that suits your property's brand image.

character sketch. A summary of a character's motivations and preferences.

Create-The-Dream. A marketing term that denotes the importance of piecing together a cohesive brand image for consumers.

consumer marketing psychology. The science and motivation behind purchasing.

content. The words and quotes you use and share.

Facebook. A social network modeled after the School Year Book; used primarily for connecting with old classmates, sharing photographs and documenting life events.

fan. A person who likes your Facebook Page.

Flickr. A social network and photo-storage site; used primarily for posting and sharing photographs and videos.

follower. A person or company who follows you on Twitter.

Hashtag. A word or phrase prefixed with the symbol #.

homepage. The page of your website that is set as the landing page or the first page you land on.

Hootsuite. A software tool that provides a dashboard overview of your social networks and allows for pre-scheduling of posts, which then post automatically at your chosen date and time.

Image. A photograph or graphic.

Klout. A measurement of engagement used to determine influence on Twitter.

keywords. Words that relate to your industry, location etc. that people will likely search for in relation to your property and which will help your page rank well in search.

navigation bar. The section of a webpage intended to help visitors easily navigate your website.

normal distribution curve. The scientific diagram which illustrates that despite the fact that groups consist of individuals there will always be a calculable average.

online connections/interactions. The people who follow you and whom you converse with online.

offline customers. Guests physically present at your property.

post. Content placed on a social network, specifically Facebook or a blog.

Pinterest. A social network designed for photo-sharing.

page. A hypertext document that forms your website. A business profile on a social network.

pre-booking. Everything leading up to a consumer booking a night at your property.

Page Insights. Statistical data pulled from your Facebook content.

photostream. A timeline image gallery of all the photographs you have uploaded to your Flickr profile.

property 'packaging'. The look and feel of your marketing; the impression and image your property exudes.

pin. An uploaded or tagged image on Pinterest.

property listing. A page on TripAdvisor dedicated to your property.

profile. A user's personal social networking page.

paid marketing. Placing advertisements and bidding on search terms in order to gain exposure and rank higher in search.

reach. The number of people your content is/can be viewed by; the extent of your viewership potential.

readership/viewership. The audience viewing your content.

ReviewAnalyst. A monitoring tool used to observe your social network activity.

screen name. The name you choose to identify yourself by online.

social network. A platform based on user-generated content.

social presence. Being present on social networks; the degree of awareness your audience has of your brand online.

social media marketing. Connecting and socializing with online connections via social networks to promote your property.

soft sell. A subtle, conversational approach to marketing and advertising.

set. An organized group of photographs on Flickr.

social calendar. An organizational method to manage your content and ensure it is on brand and consistent.

SocialOomph. A scheduling software tool that allows for pre-scheduling of posts, which then post automatically at your chosen date and time.

social ROI. The return on investment on social media marketing campaigns.

tweet. The term used to describe content posted to Twitter.

Tweetdeck. A scheduling software tool that allows the pre-scheduling of posts, which then post automatically at your chosen date and time.

Twitter timeline. A list of your Tweets in date order.

Twitter. A social network microblog that enables Tweets of 140 characters or less.

TripAdvisor. A popular travel website based on user created travel reviews.

touchpoints. The instances a guest perceives something about your property.

target audience. The people most likely to stay at your property or the type of guest you wish to attract.

username. The name you select for login identification to your online profile or page. This usually differs from your Screen name, which is public, but not in all cases such as on Pinterest.

URL. A uniform resource locator commonly referred to as a web address.

unique visitor. A person who visits a website.

website. A group of interconnected pages hosted on the world-wide web.

About The Author

Camilla Carboni is the Founder of Create-The-Dream, a marketing company focused on branding and communication tactics necessary to drive sales, and a blog dedicated to motivating others to reach their full potential.

Born and raised in South Africa, Camilla immigrated to the United States in early 2009 and launched her professional writing career shortly thereafter.

Camilla's passion for strategic, well-branded marketing naturally progressed to the online sphere as the industry developed. In early 2010 Camilla realized the power of Social Media Marketing when, using the techniques covered in this book, she salvaged a business that was under social media attack. She was then recruited by a worldwide Hospitality Company to develop the online marketing strategy and manage the social media campaign for a renowned resort, and quickly became recognized as a Social Media Specialist in the industry. Camilla coached various other properties around the globe and aided the company headquarters in compiling a Best Practice Manual.

Camilla wrote this book with the hope that it will assist and inspire everyone in the hospitality industry to join the conversation on social networks and start turning online connections into offline guests.

Camilla attended both the University of Stellenbosch in South Africa, and the University of Iowa in the U.S.A. She holds a Master's Degree in Media Reception Psychology, a Bachelor's Degree in Communications and an additional Graduate Major in English.

For more information about Camilla, please visit **camillacarboni.com**.

www.ingramcontent.com/pod-product-compliance
Lightning Source LLC
Chambersburg PA
CBHW060939050326

40689CB00012B/2505